LOVELIFE

By

SCOTT W. STROTHER

Copyright © 2019 by Scott W. Strother

All rights reserved. No portion of this book may be reproduced, stored in a retrieval system or transmitted in any form or by any means – electronic, mechanical, photocopy, recording, scanning, or other – except for brief quotations in critical reviews or articles, without the prior written permission of the publisher.

ISBN- 978-1-7326186-0-2

Unless otherwise noted, Scripture quotations are taken from the Holy Bible, New International Version, NIV. Copyright 1973,1978, 1984, 2011 by Biblica, Inc. Used by permission of Zondervan. All rights reserved worldwide. www.zondervan.com. The "NIV" and "New International Version" are trademarks registered in the United States Patent and Trademark Office by Biblica, Inc.

Scripture quotations marked as NCV are from the Holy Bible, New Century Version. Copyright 2005 by Thomas Nelson, Inc. Used by permission. All rights reserved.

Scripture quotations marked as NLT are from the Holy Bible, New Living Translation. Copyright 1996,2004, 2007, 2013, 2015 by Tyndale House Publishers, Inc., Carol Stream, Illinois 60188. All rights reserved.

Dedication

I dedicate this book to Reola, my wife and best friend. You are one of my greatest inspirations to love and I thank you for sharing in the adventure of finding greater love with the Father, Jesus, and the Holy Spirit.

Acknowledgements

Most of the thoughts in this book are not original to me but have been learned throughout the process of my life. The words are carefully and prayerfully grounded in my faith and in my study of scripture.

So, where do I begin to give credit and express thankfulness? My parents and family brought me up in faith – a very real and life-giving faith. I have been taught in Sunday school and church since birth. I graduated from three Christian universities and had many discussions with fellow students and teachers. And last, but not least, I have read and studied a lot of books, by many authors, over the years.

Thank you, Dad and Mom, Steve, and Sander. Thank you, family. Thank you, family of faith. Thank you, teachers and mentors. Thank you, John Eldredge and Ransomed Heart for correcting my course. Thank you, Danny Gill, Mark Hommel, Ed Howard, Paul Hunter, Tom Montgomery, Dean Owen, Chris Pierson, Mike Prather, Jack Skidmore and Patrick Strother for your encouragement to write, your editing and questioning, and your belief in the writer.

Thank you, Reola, Nathaniel, and Anna for your love and support! Thank you, church family for letting me stretch and grow under your grace and love.

Table of Contents

Introduction 1
Chapter 1 – The Secret of Life 5
Chapter 2 – God Loves Us First 15
Chapter 3 – Walking With God 25
Chapter 4 – The Source of Life 35
Chapter 5 – Jesus Is Proof of God's Love 43
Chapter 6 – The Holy Spirit Is More Proof 53
Chapter 7 – Beloved 63
Chapter 8 – How Is Your Lovelife? 71
Chapter 9 – False Lovers 81
Chapter 10 – Falling In Love With Jesus 91
Chapter 11 – Learning To Love 101
Chapter 12 – Words of Love 109
Chapter 13 – Worship 119
Chapter 14 – An Important Last Word 127
Notes 133

LOVELIFE

Introduction

Basic. Biblical. Life-changing. Truth.

Every new year, for the first month or so, I preach about some of the most basic and foundational truths of Christianity. I talk about God, Jesus, the Holy Spirit, the enemy, and us human beings. These are basic truths that are huge, deep, and foundational for all Christians.

I do some sermons on Jesus and the cross. I talk about the importance of knowing that we have God's Spirit living in us. I quote verses like 1 Corinthians 3:16-17, where Paul asks the Corinthian Christians, "Don't you realize that you are a dwelling place for God's Spirit?" The honest answer for most who have grown up like me is that we are not that aware and have very little understanding on the subject of the Spirit. So, I preach a sermon or two on each of these truths to try to secure some anchor points for our lives in the new year.

I talk about God and try to preach some big picture lessons on who God is, who we are in relation to God, and what God is trying to accomplish. I talk about God's plans for the world and for each individual heart. I talk about the greatest commandment and how we can grow in our love for God.

According to Jesus, the greatest and most important commandment in the Bible is to love God with all of one's heart, soul, mind, and strength. I have realized that this is a foundational and basic truth that most Christians, including myself, have not spent enough time studying and processing, much less applying

We can quote the verses. We can engage in some very religious sounding discussions on the topic. But I have learned what a novice I am at loving God just some of the time, much less with all of my heart, soul, mind, and strength.

This book has been born out of that awful discovery and my own desperate need for more life from God, much more abundant life than I have experienced to date. Learning to love God more – not religious talk, but real, honest, heart-felt love – has been powerfully opposed in my life. Honestly, it would have been easier to write a book on all the reasons that I have not loved God. Most of us, I suspect, could write quite a bit on the subjects of confusion and anger with God.

In preaching about the first and greatest commandment, I started using a word that is not found in the dictionary. It is Lovelife, with a capital L. I use the word to describe the loving relationship each of us is supposed to have with God. So, when I ask, "How is your Lovelife?", I am referring only about your relationship with God. If you don't like it, feel free not to use it.

For the most part, in this book, I am just going to quote the Bible. Most of the important ideas that I want to share come from this proven source. I read the Bible (not my first or last time) cover to cover in preparation for this writing. I also journaled every day, for over two years, documenting my journey to find and develop a relationship with a God who was always there, in my heart, in the first place ("Don't you know…" from 1 Cor. 3). In these ways and more, I have tasted of God's goodness and love and am desperate for all I can get!

This book is not five steps to having a greater relationship with God. It is not about steps. It is about relationship with God. You either want that relationship, or you don't. It can't be faked. A relationship has to be started, nurtured, and fought for throughout a lifetime. This relationship will give meaning and power to every aspect of your life. You can begin today by stepping into a loving relationship with the Father. It is the most important action of your life!

Signed,

The preacher who Jesus loves

Chapter 1 – The Secret of Life

What is your purpose?

What are you supposed to be doing with your life?

What matters the most?

Where should you focus your time, energy, and resources?

Those are some very big and important questions! Is there a secret to understanding our lives? Is there a way to know what is most important and how we should be spending our time? Is there a way to really know, to truly answer these BIG questions? Questions like these can be so overwhelming, so out of the realm of our ability to discover, that we just give up searching. They seem too hard.

I believe that there are answers. I believe God wants you to know the secret to your life and begin living purposefully to that end. God has a purpose for your life. There is a way to know who you were created to be, by God, and what you should be doing with your life. **THERE ARE** answers! Let that sink in for a moment. *God has specific purposes for your life*! God wants you to find these important answers to your life through a loving and growing relationship with Him. The Bible is full of stories about people who developed a relationship with God and found purpose and direction for their lives. That can also be your story.

Moses Offers Life to the People of Israel

I believe that God assigns Moses one of the most difficult tasks in the Old Testament. There are quite a few hard tasks given to Bible characters. Noah had to build a huge boat over a period of 100 years to float on a body of water that didn't yet exist. That was a difficult task. Abraham had to leave his hometown, his family, his friends, and travel to an unknown place. God simply told Abraham to start walking. God did not let Abraham know the destination until he arrived. That had to be hard. There are many other men and women in the Bible that were given difficult tasks. Think of Sarah, Joseph, Gideon, Samuel, David, Daniel, the prophets, and others.

I still think that Moses had the most difficult of assignments. He had to get the children of Abraham out of slavery in Egypt. That took incredible faith because the Egyptian Pharaoh, under whom the Israelites were slaves, was the most powerful king in the world. Moses was taking his life into his hands by confronting this powerful king.

That sounds hard, but Pharaoh was the easier part. The part that came afterwards was much more difficult. Moses became a single parent to 2-3 million children! He had to put up with the problems, issues, rebellions, bitterness, and anger of people that never really trusted or submitted themselves to God. They would get so bitter and angry that they would regularly choose slavery back in Egypt, over the uncertainties of trusting in God to provide for the daily necessities of life in the desert.

After 40 years of the most difficult parenting job ever, Moses gets the people to the promised land and gives them this message. It is a message about the key to life. In Deuteronomy 30:15-18, Moses offers the people the choice between life and death.

He says:

"See, I set before you today life and prosperity, death and destruction. For I command you today to love the Lord your God, to walk in his ways, and to keep his commands, decrees and laws; then you will live and increase, and the Lord your God will bless you in the land you are entering to possess. But if your heart turns away and you are not obedient, and if you are drawn away to bow down to other gods and worship them, I declare to you this day that you will certainly be destroyed. You will not live long in the land you are crossing the Jordan to enter and possess."

Moses says there is one way to live life abundantly and another way that leads to death and destruction. The key to life that Moses gives the people of Israel is to "love the Lord your God and walk in his ways." Did you hear it? Did you see it? **The key to life is to love God!** Loving God is where all the most important answers of life are to be found. Loving God is the key to understanding everything about the meaning and purpose of your life. Is that what you were expecting?

Jesus Agrees

In John 10:10, Jesus tells his followers that He is the source of abundant life. He says, "I have come that you might have life and have it more abundantly." Abundant life. If that were available, is that something that might interest you? It certainly catches my attention. If there is a place or a person that can give abundance and meaning to this life, I want it!

Jesus is the source of abundant life. In John 14:6, Jesus tells His disciples, "I am the way and the truth and the life." Since Jesus is the source of life, He knows what gives life and where to find abundant life. Jesus knows. So, when He is asked about what is the most important thing to be doing in life, we should pay close attention.

Mark 12:28-30 says:

"One of the teachers of the law came and heard them debating. Noticing that Jesus had given them a good answer, he asked him, "Of all the commandments, which is the most important?" "The most important one," answered Jesus, "is this: 'Hear, O Israel, the Lord our God, the Lord is one. Love the Lord your God with all your heart and with all your soul and with all your mind and with all your strength.'"

Jesus says that loving God, with one's whole being, is the most important activity in which anyone can be engaged. ***That is the answer!***

Loving God was the key to Moses' declaration of life to the people of Israel. Loving God, according to Jesus, is the first and greatest endeavor of any person. Loving God, simply put, is the key to life. Loving God is the purpose of life. Loving God is the source of life. Those are some big statements! Now back to our beginning questions:

What is your purpose? What are you supposed to be doing with your life? *The answer is found in loving God with all your heart, soul, mind, and strength.*

What matters the most? Where should you focus your time, energy, and resources? *Only God knows! Only in loving God will you ever know.*

What are your unique gifts and abilities? *God knows and will reveal these truths to those who love Him.*

Learning to love God with your whole being, with all you heart, soul, mind, and strength, is the key to life. It is the very purpose for which you were created. It is the source of life for all your life. Jesus says that loving God is most important.

Knowledge without relationship is not enough. Religion and theology, without love for God and relationship with God, will lead to "hellish" behavior (Matthew 23). Great acts of service, apart from loving relationship are meaningless! Paul says in 1 Corinthians 13, that anything that we do that does not come from love, especially love for God, is meaningless – it means **NOTHING!** Paul says love is most important, even greater than faith or hope. He simply says in 1 Corinthians 13:13 that love is the greatest.

What is the opposite of those statements? Not loving God is death. Not loving God, and not knowing that you were created to love God, is a life full of loneliness and meaninglessness. If you don't love God, it will be impossible to find your true purpose and meaning in life. A life without love for God is ultimately pointless and hopeless. In short, not loving God is the pathway to hell. Not loving God is separation from God and eternal separation from God is an accurate definition of hell.

The Pharisees followed the laws of Moses. They obeyed God in many parts of their lives. The Pharisees and religious leaders were at the temple and the synagogue regularly. The problem with the Pharisees was usually not their actions. It was their hearts. In Mark 7:6, Jesus told them "their hearts were far from God." In John 5:42, He told them, "You do not have the love of God in your hearts."

So, how does one learn to love God? Where does one begin? He seems so far away. It is not like you can just get in your car and go to His house and spend the day with Him. It is not like it is possible to call Him up on the phone and talk. We can't physically see or hear Him, yet, Paul tells the Athenians, in Acts 17, that God is not hard to find. He is not far from any of us. We live and move and exist in Him. He can be found if we look for Him whole-heartedly. We have to desire Him more than anything or anyone else.

The purpose of this book is to encourage every person to pursue abundant life through a loving relationship with God. Getting to know God and developing a growing, loving, intimate relationship with God will change everything. Jesus says it is the most important action of anyone's life. Are you ready to begin? This will change everything. Your very life depends on your success. The secrets of your life are the reward for your success.

LOVELIFE

Chapter 1 - Discussion Questions

1. Does every person have a unique and God-given purpose? Briefly explain your answer.

2. What were some of the problems, or issues, that kept the people of Israel from hearing Moses' last words to them?

3. Talk about what it means to love God with all of your heart, soul, mind, and strength. Are there any people that we love this much?

4. What are some ways that loving God could be the pathway to answering life's great questions?

5. Share some reasons why not loving God is the road to destruction and death. How could the Pharisees obey God, but not love God?

LOVELIFE

Chapter 2 – God Loves Us First

1 John 4:19 (NCV) "We love because God first loved us."

The truth of God's love for us sounds simple, but I believe this is the single most difficult truth for any of us to believe. We believe God loves people. But we mostly believe He loves other people more than us. We can quote verses like John 3:16 that talk of God's love. We know God loves everybody in the world, but just can't fathom how He could know me and still love me. Why is this? Why do many of you have the same struggles that I do in personalizing God's love?

Since the first and greatest commandment is to love God with your whole being, then it actually makes sense that loving God is the most opposed action in which any person can engage. The enemy does not want you to believe that God loves you and does not want you to ever trust God's good heart for you. The enemy doesn't trust the heart of God. The devil knows that if you knew how much God really loves you then it would be much easier for you to truly love God. For the above stated reasons, and more, the devil lies about the love of God in every way possible.

I want to say something that I want you to consider very carefully. This is one of the most important statements in this book. **If you believed that God has good intentions for you and that He loves you with all His heart, it would be much easier for you to love God.** Read that statement over again. Read it one more time.

My problem is that I struggle to trust God's goodness and love, especially when it comes to me, personally. I find it hard to believe that He could love me, frankly, because He knows me too well. He knows EVERYTHING about me. Surely, God is disappointed in me because of what He knows. Do you have some of the same thoughts about yourself?

Every one of us has faced situations where we chose not to trust God, for many different reasons. We did not like what God was asking of us, and so we simply decided to do things our own way. We told – we tell – the God of the universe, "NO!" We say, "God, in this situation, I think you are wrong, so I am just going to do this my way." We don't trust Him. What is good for Him does not seem to be right for us – for me. It is how Adam and Eve fell in the garden and it is how you and I regularly move away from God in our lives.

This choice AGAINST trusting God, AGAINST trusting in God's goodness and love, is the first sin in the Bible. It is a good definition for sin, period. We choose our way and not God's way. We call this self-reliance, rather than reliance on God. The Bible calls it sin.

Adam and Eve had one rule in the Garden of Eden. Don't eat from the tree of the knowledge of good and evil. One rule. One prohibition. The devil slithered up and asked Eve why it was that God had something that she was not allowed to have. In an instant, a shift took place in Eve's heart, and she quickly decided that God was not trustworthy. God was holding out. God had things that He didn't want to share and did things He didn't want to explain. Eve ate the fruit. Adam ate the fruit. All of us, except Jesus, have chosen to eat the fruit. We have all chosen to believe the lies about God. We know God's will for our lives, but there are places and situations, that we do not trust that His ways are good and loving. We doubt that He knows what He is talking about in our specific and difficult situations. So, we ignore God and do what we want to do. We tell the all-knowing, always-loving God, "NO!"

Here is the vicious cycle that I have found myself repeating throughout my life. When I don't trust God, I can't love God with all of my heart, soul, mind, and strength. When I don't love and trust God, I begin to do more and more things my way. When I do more and more things my way, I don't believe that God loves me anymore. Sin. Separation. Isolation. Death. I have repeated this scenario many times in my life, and it's likely, so have you.

This way of living always leads to isolation and pain. This chosen way of life without God – a way that is chosen because we don't trust in God's goodness and love - is the path to sin and destruction. We must repent and change our ways. We need to trust God before we can learn to love Him. Here is a Biblical truth that should help.

An Essential Biblical Truth

There is a phrase that is repeated many times in the bible. It affirms two truths about God that are necessary for us to believe if we are to learn to love God. They are found together in some of King David's most beloved songs. In 1 Chronicles 16:34, David says, "Give thanks to the Lord, for he is good; his love endures forever." Did you see the two phrases? The first phrase is "God is good." The second is "God's love endures forever." If we believed these two truths it would be easier for us to love God. So, a foundational and Biblical starting place to begin to love God with all one's heart is faith that God is good and full of love for people.

False religion can take these two truths in some weird directions. For instance, words have one meaning in our everyday lives, but then we redefine those words when we are talking about God. Love is one of those words. We know what it means to say, "I love my wife," or "I love my kids." But when we say, "I love God," it can mean a lot of different things. Do you love God in the same way that you love your spouse, kids, or a best friend? Well… not exactly. God is not like a person that you can touch and see and relate to "face to face." For some people, loving God might simply mean that they go to church or pray on occasion. A lot of people say that they love God just because they know that is the right answer. But for the most part, they don't really know and trust Him enough to have "deep down in their heart" loving feelings for God. Some of you might not even believe that loving God in the same way you love family and friends is possible. God feels too distant and uninvolved in your life.

LOVELIFE

Jesus says that loving God is the single most important of all God's commands that are mentioned in the Bible. Love God. Really. Love God from the depths of your heart - from the bottom of your feet to the top of your head. We are to love God more than we love our spouses, children, and friends. We are to have more affection and more desire for relationship with Him than anyone or anything else in life. Is this command possible? Do you know anyone who loves God this way? I know one. Jesus. The rest of us either don't believe it is possible or we are somewhere in the process of attaining this love for God.

I want to share one more story from the Bible. In the Old Testament, one of the great lovers of God was King David. David loved God so much that he wanted to do something special for God. David wanted to move God's dwelling place out of the tent of Moses and into a beautiful temple. David prepared all the building materials for the temple of God, and then David's son Solomon was the one who was allowed, by God, to build it.

At first glance, this all seems exciting and wonderful. But the reality of having the all-powerful, holy God living in the middle of a rebellious and sinful nation was terrifying! In Exodus 20, trembling and terror is the overwhelming experience of the people of Israel when they were led by Moses through the desert to Mt. Sinai and to God's Presence.

So much happened between God and mankind from the Garden of Eden to the building of the temple. The chasm that was now between God and man, because of sin and rebellion, was enormous! The law, delivered by Moses, had only made the gulf bigger. Was close relationship with God even possible? Was there any bridge that could span this terrible chasm?

The Apostle John says that there is one trait of God that is descriptive of His very essence. In 1 John 4:8, John writes very simply, "God is love." God is love. God is the real definition of love. God is love and is the originator of all love. Hollywood did not introduce the world to love. Poets did not invent love. The sellers of Valentine's Day chocolates and cards did not come up with the idea of love. God did. God is love!

What gave Solomon and the people of Israel the courage to invite the Holy God into their midst? ***They found comfort and courage in God's love!*** In 2 Chronicles 5, scripture tells us that while they were bringing the Ark of the Covenant (the earthly throne where His Presence dwelled!) into the temple, they were singing a song of David, and repeating it over and over. "He is good; His love endures forever! God is good; His love endures forever!!" There were musicians, singers, cymbals, harps, lyres, trumpets; everybody was singing and pronouncing in unison, in faith, "God is good. His love endures forever."

Then it gets terrifying! God shows up in 2 Chronicles 7! He shows up in such a powerful and dramatic a way that even all the people outside of the building see His Holy Fire descending into the temple. What did they do? They fell with their faces to the ground, and worshiped God saying, "He is good; His love endures forever."

God is infinitely difficult to describe. He is awesome in His Holiness. He is an impartial and just judge. He is powerful beyond description. He is all of these things and infinitely more besides. Most important for us, the good news throughout history is that He is eternally good and forever full of love for all His children. Yes, that includes you!

LOVELIFE

Chapter 2 - Discussion Questions

1. Has it ever been difficult for you to trust that God likes you, that God really loves you? Talk about some of the reasons for your answer.

2. "If you believed God was completely good and really loved you, it would be easier for you to love Him." Share some reasons why you agree or disagree with this statement.

3. What are some reasons why self-reliance, rather than reliance on God, demonstrates a lack of trust in God?

4. What does it mean to you that one of the most common descriptions of God in the Bible is, "He is good and His loves endures forever."?

5. What would you be thinking about if you knew that you were about to personally, face-to-face, meet the Holy, All Knowing, All Powerful, God? Would it help to know that God is good and full of love for all His children?

Lovelife

Chapter 3 – Walking With God

If the most important thing that we can do in life is to love God with all our being, then it makes sense to say that the reason we were created is to live in a loving relationship with God. We were created to live, to make sense of our lives, in the context of a loving relationship with our Heavenly Father.

Even if we know this is a Biblical truth, it is hard to figure out how to put "loving God" into practice. If a loving relationship with God is so important, then why does this seem like one of the hardest things to do? We have already said that the enemy knows how important our Lovelife with God is, so, it really does make sense that all the powers of hell fight against this relationship. The enemies of God hate people that love God.

LOVELIFE

I spent a couple of years preaching through the Old Testament books of Genesis and Exodus, in the church where I serve. One of the obvious themes of these first books, which describe God's first interactions with the first people, is the lack of relationship most had with God. For most people, there was none. The desire of people for relationship with God has been historically pitiful and untrusting. The central stories of the Bible demonstrate the impressive lengths to which God will go to be in relationship with anyone who is willing. God's pursuit of human hearts is one of the great themes of all the stories in Genesis and Exodus, and in the rest of the Bible.

Adam and Eve, because of their sinful choice, were banished from the Garden of Eden and from daily communion with God in the Garden. God did not want sinful people, now with eyes fully open to all the possibilities of selfish and sinful actions, to be able to eat from the tree of life and live forever as sin sick beings (Genesis 3:22). Because of sin, they were now going to die. Because of sin, they needed to die. Sinful people need to know that they cannot do whatever they want against God and others, with absolutely no consequences to themselves. Sinful actions have always had deadly consequences. In fact, violence and bloodshed filled the thoughts and activities of the first people very quickly. So,

God made a very difficult decision. Men and women would not be allowed to be their own little gods and still live under the blessing and healing of the One True God.

Adam and Even sinned and were removed from the Garden. Cain killed his brother Abel because he refused to master the jealousy and anger that was in his heart. Cain killed his brother and hoped that God would not notice. He hoped to get away with murder. God banished Cain even farther away, farther from relationship with God and men, because he had chosen (even more than his parents) to do things his own way.

Another son was born to Adam and Eve, named Seth. During his time, some of the people began to call out for God, to call on the name of the Lord (Gen. 4:26). Something relational was beginning between sinful mankind and God, but it was much less relationship than was available at first, in the garden.

The beginning of Genesis, chapter 5, makes it clear that we were created to be God's children. We were not created to be God's science experiments, or His bug collection, but we were created to be the Heavenly Father's beloved children. God created us in His likeness, the same way that Seth had children that were born in his likeness (Genesis 5:3). These Genesis 5 verses promote the idea that there could have been a much more "family-like" relationship between God and man than what took place. Not much has changed throughout history.

The rest of Genesis 5 goes over the genealogy of mankind from Adam to Noah. Out of all these men and their sons, there are only two that seem to merit special mention. The two men are Enoch and Noah. In Genesis 5, a very interesting phrase is used about Enoch. He is the first person in the Bible to be mentioned in this special way. This phrase is found in Genesis 5:22 and is then repeated in Genesis 5:24. It is short and very intriguing. The Bible says, "Enoch walked with God."

Enoch walked with God. What does that mean? Is it a reference to an exercise program in which God and Enoch were mutually involved? No. It is about much more than walking for exercise. This phrase was used to describe people in the Bible who had a growing and intimate relationship with God. These people were known as God's friends.

People who walked with God were unique individuals that desired to have relationship with God and be God's friends. How simple and beautiful. There have always been people (children of God), that have wanted to have more relationship with God, that have wanted to walk through life **WITH** God. This is the kind of person I want to be. These are the kind of people that I am trying to find and encourage through this book. There is more available in your relationship with God. You were created for more. In fact, ***it was the purpose of God for your creation!*** He wants to share in a loving relationship with you. He wants to walk with you!

Before we go any further, I need to mention a much larger group of people in the Bible. Most people from the beginning of creation have NOT chosen to follow God. They have NOT chosen to walk with God. They didn't want to be God's friends. There were many reasons for making this choice in their lives. A few of the reasons were things like pain and suffering, selfishness, anger and bitterness, hatred, and jealousy. These people blamed God for the results of their own bad choices. They chose something other than God and God's way and then got mad at God when their choices had hard consequences. So, people, who were created to be God's children, chose not to be known as God's children. Children who were created to live in loving relationship with the Father, angrily chose relationship with someone or something else. Sometimes, in their anger and frustration, they chose against relationship altogether.

This choice against relationship with God seems like it would be the exception. Sadly, it has been the prevailing choice of mankind since the beginning of time. God really does let people choose. Through bad choices and by believing the lies of the enemy, most people have chosen against relationship with God. My prayer and aim are that you and I will not be like those people, but that we will be like the examples of those men and women who chose to walk with God.

Adam and Eve knew God and had relationship with him in the Garden. Seth called on God. Enoch and Noah walked with God. Abraham, Isaac, and Jacob walked with God. Joseph walked with God and relied on God's leading all his life. Even Sarah's slave Hagar had a large part of a chapter devoted to her in Genesis 16, because she called on God in her anguish and distress. Hagar gave God one of the most beautiful names in scripture. She said, "God is the God who sees me." God is the God who was willing to be involved in the life of a despised and worthless slave woman, like Hagar. She wanted more relationship with this God. What about you?

Abraham, Joseph, Moses, Joshua, Samuel, David, Daniel, and others were not only men who walked with God, but they were known as friends of God. They spent so much time with Him that they considered God to be a faithful and personal friend. Oh, you can be sure that they understood elements of danger and fear in their relationship with Almighty God, but they also knew Him as a trusted and intimate friend. They, and a few others like them, are held up in the Bible as the examples of people who pleased God and who lived under His goodness and blessings. Most chose against God.

Because of the loving relationship the friends of God had, they were protected and blessed like very few in the whole world. Abraham's enemies became God's enemies. Isaac and Jacob were blessed and protected because of their desire to walk with God in their lives. Moses' brother and sister found out that to rebel against their brother Moses, God's friend, was almost the same thing as rebelling against God himself. Moses did not have to defend himself, because God was there to defend him instantly (you can read the story in Numbers 12).

This was also true for the whole nation of Israel. If Israel chose friendship with God, then He would choose them and bless them like no other nation on earth. But when they chose not to walk with God, then the stories about the nation of Israel quickly got hard and messy.

The central stories of the Bible are about the men and women who chose to walk with God. These are the stories of Joshua and Caleb; of the judges like Deborah and Samuel; of good and faithful kings like David and Hezekiah; of the prophets like Elijah and Daniel; and anyone else who would call on God and invite Him into their lives. God's involvement in the lives of those who became His loving friends was a powerful force indeed. I believe that this is still true today for those who lovingly walk with God, for those who are learning to love God and be a friend of God. I want that to be my story. I hope you will choose intimate friendship with God to be the central part of your life story. May you be one that walks with God for the rest of your life!

LOVELIFE

Chapter 3 – Discussion Questions

1. You were created for the very purpose of living in a loving relationship with God. Discuss this statement in your group.

2. Talk about some of the reasons why you believe that most people never develop a loving relationship with God.

3. What does it mean to you to think of being one of God's beloved children versus one of his experiments or projects?

4. What do you believe it took for Enoch to become a person who walked with God? What would it take for the same to be said about you?

5. As you are becoming a friend of God, what are some things about you or your life that are changing?

Lovelife

Chapter 4 – The Source of Life

Loving God is not only the purpose for which we were created, but, having a loving relationship with God is the very source of life. **GOD IS THE SOURCE** of life!

Let me take a moment to explain what I mean. How many sources of electricity do you have in your home? Some folks might go around and count the plugs in every room. We know that all our appliances and electrical gadgets need to be "plugged in" to work. A refrigerator does not keep food cold and preserved for long if it is not plugged into a power source.

So, plugs are the power sources in our homes. No. A plug, or electrical outlet, without being wired into "something more" is dead and useless. So, wires are the source of power. No. Wires, by themselves, contain no electrical power. The wires in your home must be connected to the power lines outside of your home. Those electrical lines have to go to an actual power plant for them to work. The real power sources are the coal plants, nuclear plants, or water and wind plants that provide power for every light bulb and electrical appliance in our homes. Power plants provide electricity. Everything else ***uses*** electricity.

We live in an age of very powerful batteries that run everything from cell phones to cars. In a way, these batteries are a temporary source of power. But all of these still have to be "plugged into a source" or charged from a much bigger and truer source of energy.

God is the **one and only** source of power. In Acts 17, Paul is in Athens, Greece and talking to the people about the One True God that created everything. He tells the people, that don't yet know God, that God is so big and powerful and present that we all "live and move and have our being" in Him. That is a description of God as the source. God is the beginning place of life and the abiding place of all life. God is the originator and the source of life. He is the source of life for all of us as we live and move and have our being on this earth.

Where do you go to find life? There are so many things, places, and people that look like sources of life. Some of them even claim to be sources of life. The problem is that they

never live up to their claims. They are not sources. Because they are not true sources, *they are users*. Users will drain you and, ultimately, destroy you if you go to them as a source for power in your life. They will steal and use the precious power for life that you currently have stored within yourself. Are you hearing what I am saying? Food is not a true source of life. Sex is not a true source of life. When they are connected to **THE SOURCE (God),** then and only then, can they have real power to give into your life. But if they are not connected to God, then they are false sources and will end up stealing your very life. Jesus says in John 10:10 that he came to give abundant life. Jesus, God in the flesh, is a real source of life. But Jesus says that there are thieves, or false gods, that steal, kill, and destroy. You and I need to be connected to the True Source, our Heavenly Father, His Son, and His Spirit.

A few years ago, I came up with an idea to show the difference between a source of power and something that only uses power. I searched the internet shopping sites for a small ceramic indoor fountain that had a mill and a water wheel. I found a small one that looked very real. It had a small pump that would circulate water and make the water wheel turn. I set it up to be a beautiful table ornament and used it in some teaching situations. It was pretty. It was nice. People liked the way it looked, worked, and even the sound that the water made as it worked its way around the small fountain. This small water wheel looked like the real thing and even functioned similarly to the real thing, but it was a fake and a lie. A real water wheel uses flowing water as a source of power and energy. The real water wheel can be a source of power to a mill or factory. The fake water wheel is a user. It must be plugged in to a wall to even work! I hope you are getting the point.

There is one true source of life: God. There are many fake sources, false gods, that steal, kill, and destroy. How many false sources of life do you have? Where are the places and who are the people to which you go for times of refreshing and renewal, other than God? Most of us have so many false gods that it is hard to answer this question and recognize the lies. False gods are **never** a source of life, they are thieves and destroyers of life. False gods are stone cold killers! They are all from the enemy.

So, again, how many "false sources" do you have in your life? When life gets hard, do you turn to God or to chocolate? When life is confusing and painful, do you seek God, or do you try to escape through sports, sex, hobbies, shopping, sleeping, or going somewhere to hide and relax? Anything or anyone else, other than God, is a false god, a **user** of your life energy. God is the one and only source of life. Jesus is the source of abundant life.

Since most people are not connected to or "plugged into" God, they do not have a real source of life and power in their lives. Most people don't really understand the God-given glory and power for their lives. Even less do they believe that there is a God-created purpose for their lives. Life most often feels random and meaningless. It feels powerless. If you and I are going to find real power for life, we are going to have to find it in relationship with our Heavenly Father.

What difference would it make in your life if you believed you had the power to accomplish anything? Philippians 4:13 says that you can do anything through the strength that Jesus gives to you. What if you believed this truth and knew you were connected to Jesus in a way that would give you power to accomplish anything, according to His will? That is the message of Paul in Philippians 4:13!

The good news is that God is powerful and able to give you all you need to accomplish His purpose in your life. **He is the source of life-giving power!**

One of my favorite verses in scripture that talks about this is Philippians 2:13 (NCV), which says to Christians, "God is working in you to help you want to do and be able to do what pleases him." If you believe that God loves you and wants good things for your life, then it is comforting to know that He is working in you to give you purpose and power.

Are you plugged into God? If not, it is no wonder that you feel empty and lost! God is the source. Jesus is the way, the truth, and the life. Jesus' Spirit is called a life-giving Spirit in 1 Corinthians 15:45.

Your loving relationship with God and your walking in daily, regular relationship with Him is the only source of real power and meaning. Your loving relationship with God is the key to finding the purpose of your existence. Your loving relationship with God is the key to finding the power to fulfill your purpose. That is why loving God with all your heart, mind, soul, and body is most important. It is the only way to get plugged in and to stay plugged in to The Power, which is God. Having power in your life depends on a life-giving connection to God the Father, God the Son, and God the Holy Spirit!

LOVELIFE

Chapter 4 - Discussion Questions

1. Talk about the differences between a "source" of power and a "user" of power.

2. What are some false sources of life that you have tried to use?

3. How are your false gods working for you? Do they give life or steal life? Discuss your answers.

4. What do you think are some of the reasons that we don't turn to God for life?

5. Walking with God and loving God is plugging yourself into the true source of everything good in life. Discuss this statement in your group.

LOVELIFE

Chapter 5 – Jesus Is Proof of God's Love

In 1 John 4:7 (NCV), John says that "God is love." As proof of God's love, the Apostle John says, in vv. 9-10, that "He (God) sent his one and only Son into the world so that we could have life through him." Jesus is proof of God's love. John states this truth clearly in John 3:16, "For God so loved the world that he gave his one and only Son, that whoever believes in him shall not perish but have eternal life." How much does God love you? God loved you so much that He sent His Son into the world to give you life. You and I were dying in the self-imposed isolation and self-created destructive patterns of our self-made worlds. We chose a life of sin. We claimed our rights to do what we wanted, we made ourselves "god" and ignored the God who created us. God rescued us by sending His Son into the world to give us the chance for eternal life.

How does Jesus give life and save people from their sins? The answer is very "Old Testament." It takes some understanding of the Old Testament to make sense of both the question and the answer. Here is a short version. In the garden, with just Adam and Eve, God tells the first humans that when they sin by disobeying God's rules, that from that moment they will die. Death will become a reality in the world when sin happens. They sin. They begin to die. The Bible makes it clear that sin, rebellion against God and His way of life, quickly becomes the rule and the norm for people. We read in Genesis 6:5, "The Lord saw how great man's wickedness on the earth had become, and that every inclination of the thoughts of his heart was only evil all the time." This is one of the saddest descriptions of people in the Bible. They were plotting and carrying out evil all the time, 7 days a week, 365 days a year!

Sin is so completely the norm by the time of Noah that all the people of the world live in sin and death, with a continual selfish desire for more. All people who have ever lived deserve to die and are dying because of their sinful (*full of sin*) lives. The Old Testament law, including the Ten

Commandments, only increases the scope of sin. Now, because of God's written law, people cannot claim ignorance of God's will. God begins to teach Abraham's children, the children of Israel, just how serious and deadly is a life of chosen rebellion against Him. For thousands of years, in the Jewish temple and sacrificial system, Jewish people participated in animal sacrifices for their sins. They had to place their hand on the head of the animal, while it was being killed, as a sacrifice to pay for their sin. They proclaimed in this visual, participatory, and "bloody" manner, "My sin caused this death."

When Jesus appears on the scene to begin his earthly ministry, John the Baptist declares in John 1:29, "Look, the Lamb of God, who takes away the sin of the world." Jesus is going to be the sacrificial lamb that pays the penalty for our sins. Jesus dies the death that we deserve to die for our sin and rebellion against God. Jesus dies on the cross, for us, so that we don't have to die for our own sins. In 1 John 4:14, John says that Jesus' death on the cross is for every human in the whole world. It reads, "And we have seen and testify that the Father has sent his Son to be the Savior of the world."

Did you hear it? Did you apply it to yourself? The amazing part of this declaration of God's love is that it covers every single human being that has ever lived, beginning with Adam and Eve, all the way to you and me, and then into the future. Did you hear the words and apply them to yourself? God's love, demonstrated through Jesus, is for you. How do I know? Because John says that God sent his son to be the Savior of the whole world; ***every single person in the whole world!*** That includes you and me.

This precise wording of Jesus as the Savior of the world is found in one other place in the New Testament (though the idea is found in many places). But the exact wording is in one other place. It is in John's gospel, the 4th chapter, in the story about Jesus and the Samaritan woman.

This is such a beautiful story and one that makes a very bold statement about God's love, in Jesus. Samaritans were "half–breed" Jews. When God brought the people of Moses into the promised land, he did not want the Jewish people to intermarry with the non-Jewish people in the lands that God was giving to them. The problem was that the godlessness and immorality of these "non-Jews" was so great that the people of Israel would be led into all kinds of idolatry and sin through their associations with these other nations. So, God made it a very serious issue for the Jewish people NOT to make alliances of any kind with these nations (read Deut. 7). God wanted His people to be a holy nation, a pure nation, a nation that was set apart from all the other Godless people of the world. Under the law of Moses, Samaritans did not have any chances to be reconciled to the Jewish nation. All that changed with Jesus. He came to be the Savior of Jews, Samaritans, and Gentiles (Gentiles are everybody that is not a Jew or Samaritan). Jesus is the Savior of everybody in the world!

So, in John 4, Jesus and His apostles were traveling from Judea to Galilee. John 4:4 says that they had to go through Samaria on the way. A lot of Jews would simply go around Samaria. Jesus went through Samaria, and He stopped in the village of Sychar. He was tired. He wanted to rest. He sent His followers away to get food while He rested near Jacob's well. A Samaritan woman came to the well during the heat of the day (a time that no other people would be there), and Jesus engaged her in conversation. This is a scandalous and very unexpected story in scripture for anybody living in New Testament times. Since the Old Testament seemed to write these people off, the Jewish people had written these people off. The Samaritans were beyond saving because of the nature and scope of their sin.

Jesus knew these rules, but His love and mission extended beyond the Old Testament rules in a way that nobody at the time could imagine. Jesus demonstrated His love and forgiveness of this broken, hopeless, and helpless Samaritan woman. To prove that He had the power and authority to forgive this woman, Jesus revealed to the woman and the other Samaritans that He was the Messiah. This is something that He does not even do with most of the Jewish faithful. He revealed Himself to the Samaritans to prove that He had the desire and the authority to be their Savior. When He leaves this region, the Samaritan people call Jesus "the Savior of the world (John 4:42)!" What an awesome and compelling description!

If Jesus is willing and able to save Samaritans, then Jesus can save anybody in the world. Let that statement sink in for a moment. In most people's minds, during the time of Jesus, it would be easier for the Jews to think about Gentiles being saved before considering the possibility that Samaritans could be saved. The Gentiles were, at least, sinning out of a total lack of knowledge and lack of relationship with God. The Samaritans used to be Jews. They didn't have any excuse for the failure and disobedience in their lives. So, if the Messiah, Jesus, was willing to offer them forgiveness and restore them to relationship with God, then Jesus is, indeed, the Savior of the whole world! How awesome! How beautiful! How BIG is God's love for the whole world! Jesus came to prove the unfathomable love of God, for all people, by becoming the Savior of the whole world.

Jesus is proof of God's love for you. Because it is so hard for you and me to personalize the truth of God's love, He sent us Jesus. Immanuel is one of the scriptural names of Jesus that is found in the Old Testament (Isaiah 7:14 and 8:8). It was a name given to Jesus at his birth, as noted in Matthew 1:23, "...they will call him Immanuel, which means "God with us."

God often "feels" so far away and uninvolved in our lives. Jesus, Immanuel, our God who is with us, reveals in the boldest way possible God's love for each of us. Jesus is proof of God's love for you because He died as your Savior. You. Personally. But you must accept God's offer of love.

How do you accept His offer? Well, just like the Samaritan woman, you must let Jesus come into your life. Jesus is the Savior of the world, but He can be rejected by any who don't want Him, who don't want to admit their brokenness and neediness. You must accept Jesus as your Savior and let Him be Lord of your life. Faith is the starting place.

Many of us are still playing the games of the Samaritan woman, before her encounter with Jesus. We think we are hiding our sin and brokenness from others. We even think we are hiding from God. We live our lives desperately hoping others are not aware of our sin and brokenness. Remember, the Samaritan woman was getting her water in the hottest part of the day, just so she wouldn't have to talk to anyone. But Jesus knew everything about her life and still went out of His way to meet her and rescue her heart and life.

Jesus knows everything about you also. He knows all your secrets. He knows that you are afraid that you will never be loved and can't be saved. Jesus is the Savior of the whole world. That includes you. That includes all your failures and sins. Jesus is proof of God's love for you. The God who loves you this much is worthy of all your love!

Chapter 5 - Discussion Questions

1. Does Jesus feel like proof of God's love for you? Discuss your answer.

2. Why did Jesus have to die on a cross for you and me? Do you believe that you need Jesus to be a sacrifice for your sins? Explain.

3. Like the Samaritan woman, how is Jesus trying to seek you and save you from your sin, isolation, and death?

4. Talk about the statement, "If Jesus can save a Samaritan, then He can save anyone."

5. What does it mean to you that Jesus knows everything about you, every hidden struggle and sin, and still loves you and wants to be your Savior?

LOVELIFE

Chapter 6 – The Holy Spirit Is More Proof

1 John 4:12-13 says, "No one has ever seen God: but if we love one another, God lives in us and his love is made complete in us. We know that we live in him and he in us, because he has given us of his Spirit."

We know that God lives in us and his love is made complete in us because he has given us His Spirit. That is such a strange statement, even for many Christians. I know many in my life who have been faithful servants of God for many years, but who still don't know how to grasp how the Spirit of God lives in them. Even though this is hard, the presence of God's Spirit is a very important truth to understand if we are to really appreciate how much God loves us.

I have a Sunday School question for you. How many people either saw or touched God in the Old Testament?

Adam and Eve had personal and visual contact with God, but after the first sin, the answer is "Nobody!" No one in the sinful world has seen God face to face (John 1:18) or touched him (it is possible that Jesus did, but we are not told for sure).

Why does contact between God and people diminish in the Bible? Because God is perfect. God is perfectly holy. God does not sin or have intimate relationship with sinful people. Sinful people are separated from God. Adam and Eve were forced out of the Garden of Eden. After Adam and Eve, personal contact with God became non-existent and all communication from God happened from a much greater distance. It took place through a mediator, like an angel or a prophet. Scripture points out that God did not actually talk to Moses from the burning bush, rather it was an angel (Exodus 3:2).

When Moses and the children of Israel met with God at Mt. Sinai, God gave Moses and the people very clear instructions about how close any persons or animals were allowed to get to the mountain where God was present. Only Moses and Joshua were allowed to go inside of the roped off boundaries of the mountain. Anybody or any animal that went beyond the boundary was to be put to death. They were to be stoned or shot with arrows. Nobody was allowed to touch the people or animals that had touched the mountain where the Holy and Almighty God was present.

There are other examples of boundaries between God and man after sin comes into the world. There were angels with flaming swords that blocked the way to the Garden of Eden. When the Tabernacle was set up in the midst of Israel, the rules became much more restrictive as anyone got closer to the Holy of Holies, where God was present. Even the first and greatest high priest Aaron, Moses' brother, had very strict instructions for when and how (on penalty of death!) he could go into the Most Holy Place, because God's Presence was over the Ark (Leviticus 16:1-2). Aaron's sons Nadab and Abihu were killed for not honoring God's Holiness while serving in the Tabernacle. Even when God allowed the Tabernacle to be raided and plundered because of Israel's sin and unfaithfulness, the Ark of the Covenant was frightening and deadly for any nation that took it away for its value in gold. They sent it back quickly, with all the gold still attached, because of their fear of the God of Israel (1 Samuel 5:11)!

So, after men and women became sinful, the distance between God and mankind grew bigger. Mankind became less and less dedicated (holy) to God. It is very important to note that this was not God's original purpose or goal. Throughout the books of Genesis and Exodus (throughout all history), God has looked for men and women who would make the effort to "walk with Him," or "call on Him." God has always wanted more relationship with His children, but our sin and rejection of Him as God and Father made relationship difficult (it felt impossible) for most human beings. We chose, and often still choose, to do our own thing and live apart from Him. He chooses to let us.

Here is some good news. God's plan has always been reconciliation with his children. God has always wanted relationship with His children to be restored. The difficulty of reconciliation with God is a problem of Biblical proportions! How does a Holy God become reconciled, or brought in closer relationship, with un-holy, sinful people? 2 Corinthians 5:11-21 talks about this problem and God's solution in detail. ***There is only one way. Jesus.***

John 3:16 says that God loved the world, the people in the world, so much that He sent his one and only Son so that everyone who believes in Jesus could have eternal life. God's desire is for all people to believe and to be saved through Jesus' death on the cross. Jesus had to take away our sins, give us His holiness and righteousness, so that something very amazing could happen.

LOVELIFE

Here it is. Through the holiness and righteousness of Jesus, which is given to us when we put our faith in Him, we are reconciled in our relationship to God. This is a staggering truth. Through Jesus, we can touch God. He touches us. Through the Holy Spirit, God comes to live in the heart of every faithful believer in Jesus. Followers of Jesus are given the beautiful gift of God's Presence in their lives, dwelling with them in their bodies. We can have a fully restored, intimate relationship with God. Christians not only walk with God, but through the Holy Spirit, they become one with God!

God loves us so much that He was willing to sacrifice the life of His Perfect Son so that we could be reconciled to Him. When we are reconciled to God through Jesus, then and only then can His Spirit come to live with us, to dwell inside of us. Acts 2:38 says this is true for every Christian, from the first to the last. God loves us so much that He has made it possible for us to live with Him, talk with Him, be in relationship with Him "every moment of every day" for the rest of our lives! Now that is amazing! That kind of love is awesome! That kind of love inspires greater love from my heart to my Loving Father.

In 1 Corinthians 3:16 – 17 and 1 Corinthians 6:19, Paul asks the believers a very important question. He asks, "Don't you know that you are a dwelling place for God's Spirit? Don't you know that He lives in you?" So, do you know? Ask yourself. Check your heart. Do you know that God's Spirit lives in you? If you are a Christian, then you have been reconciled to God through Jesus, and it is God's desire to live in intimate relationship with you. He lives and works in your body. What does this incredible teaching do for your heart? It speaks a powerful message of love and grace to me. God wants to be with me always! This is not just a promise for heaven or a promise for someday. It is reality for Christians here and now.

How much relationship with God is possible? That is a question for you that only you can answer. It is up to you. If you are in Christ, God's Spirit already lives in your heart. He is always there. He is always present, and it is now up to you to make yourself present with Him.

There is a beautiful Christian song which describes how this relationship works. It is called "On and On," written and sung by the group Tenth Avenue North.

> Love, I have waited for you
> And love, I was wounded for you
> Won't you look into my eyes
> Through the pain and through your pride
> And find I am true?
>
> You're the one I can't deny,

LOVELIFE

And I'll never leave your side
I gave my life for you, So what are you waiting for?

On and on we go, Come love take my hand
On and on we go, Time and time again
On and on we go, Back to where this all began
Come love take my hand.

Life is waiting for you
And life I have given to you
Tell me what else can I do
What more have I left to prove?
That I am what you need.

Still I will hold onto your heart,
Through the chaos and the dark
When your eyes fail to see, So what are you waiting for?

On and on we go, Well, come love, take my hand
On and on we go, As you turn away again
On and on we go, Back to where this all began
Broken I was for you, Broken I'm still for you
My broken heart breaks for you, Broken I'm over you[1]

In this song, Jesus is talking to you. You are God's beloved. In this song, your name is "love." Put your name every place it says love. Jesus, through His Spirit, is inviting you into relationship. God has done everything necessary, through Jesus, to reestablish intimate relationship with you. The rest is up to you. How far will you go into this relationship?

In Christ, we have been reconciled to God. Through Christ's work, you and I have become dwelling places for God's Spirit. Intimate relationship with God is the goal. God has done this out of incredible love for you and me. Will you give your heart, in love, to Him and go deeper into relationship?

LOVELIFE

Chapter 6 - Discussion Questions

1. What are some of the reasons why the people of Israel were not allowed to touch Mt. Sinai in Exodus 19?

2. God wants to be reconciled to you and all His children. What does this say about God's heart?

3. Acts 2:38 says that the gift of God's Spirit is for every single believer – then and now. What do you think about this statement?

4. Do you know that God has given you His Spirit to live in your heart? What are some ways you have experienced the Spirit?

5. What kind of relationship with God is possible if His Spirit always lives in your heart?

Lovelife

Chapter 7 – Beloved

Could you put your name for the name "love" in the song, "On and On" in the previous chapter? Do you believe that God really loves you? Jesus is proof of God's love for you. The Holy Spirit, living in you, is more proof of God's love for you. There are also the many words, in the Bible, that God uses to address the people that He loves. We are going to look at a few of these names, or descriptions, that God has for His children.

When we talk to our loved ones, we often have pet names or loving names that are reserved for those whom we hold most dear to our hearts. We use words like, dear, sweetheart, darling, my love, etc. God also uses some of these special names and special expressions of love for His children. I hope that these will give you confidence in God's love for you so that you can grow more in your heartfelt love for your Heavenly Father.

In Ephesians 5:1, we are called God's beloved children. ***You are God's beloved son or daughter!*** We are not His bug collection. We are not His science experiment. We are definitely not the greatest mistake of His creation. People are the very purpose of His creation. We are His centerpiece, His masterpiece. This truth is so assaulted by the enemy that many of you have never heard this and some of you can't believe it, especially about yourselves. You are God's beloved daughter. You are God's beloved son. Did you know that in John 17:26, Jesus says that God loves us in the same way that He loves Jesus? Let those words sink in for a moment. God loves you with the same love that He has for His son Jesus. Can you believe that? What would it take for you to trust Jesus' words?

All people are God's beloved children. God loves every single one of His children. It is why God continually puts so much emphasis on people and how we treat other people. They all matter to Him. We all matter to Him. God loves us so much that He would send His perfect child to rescue all His "not-so-perfect" and very lost children. John 3:16-17 (ESV) says it this way, "For God so loved the world, that he gave his only Son, that whoever believes in him should not perish but have eternal life. For God did not send his Son into the world to condemn the world, but in order that the world might be saved through him." "The world" is referring to all the people of the world. That includes you.

What difference would it make in your ability to love God with all your heart if you knew, really knew, that He loves you? You are His beloved son or daughter. You are (fill in your name), God's beloved son or daughter. We love God because He first loved us. Remember 1 John 4:19! It is much easier to love God when you know how much He loves you.

God created you with glorious intent. You were created in the image of your Father. 2 Corinthians 3:18, says that in Jesus we become increasingly like our glorious Father. We begin to look like our True Father. I am not talking about your earthly mother and father, but your Heavenly Father. He created you with something wonderful in mind. He created you for good. He created you because of His love for you. How would your life change if you believed these words? What difference would it make in the way you treated others, if you believed these words?

Not only are we loved as God's children, but we are loved as the bride of Christ, the bride of God. James 4:5 talks about this reality. When we chase other lovers and follow "little g" gods, it doesn't just make God angry. It breaks His heart. He loves you the way that a husband loves his wife, or a wife loves her husband. When we don't live in loving relationship with God and have Him as the greatest love of our lives, it breaks His heart. He considers that to be something like adultery. It feels like we are being unfaithful to Him. James 4:5 (NCV) says, "Do you think the Scripture means nothing that says, "The Spirit that God made to live in us wants us for himself alone"?" You are God's beloved! You are the desire of His heart! He loves you passionately! It feels like adultery to Him when we don't recognize His love and go after other lovers.

What if you woke up every morning and thought, "God passionately desires relationship with me today, every moment of this day?" He likes me. He loves me. He loves spending time with me. He loves talking with me about anything and everything. Everything in my life matters to Him. Have you ever thought of your relationship with God in this light?

Once you begin to believe that God loves you, then many more of the descriptions that are in the Bible begin to jump off the page. In Genesis and Exodus, God is looking for anyone that will walk in relationship with Him through life. God is looking for friends. Seth walked with God. Enoch walked with God so fully that God took him away to be with Him forever. Noah walked with God. Abraham was God's friend. Moses was God's friend. David was passionate about his lovelife with God and became a man after God's own heart. Most people throughout history have not chosen to have any relationship with God. But for those that are looking, relationship is available and the source of true life.

One of the ways to summarize the Bible, is that it is the story of God's pursuit of relationship with all His children. In John 1:12, John the apostle says that through the work of Jesus, all people can come back into relationship with God. That is what God wants. That is what Jesus died for on the cross, so that we could be reconciled into relationship with God. Paul summarized his ministry, in 2 Corinthians 5, as a ministry of reconciliation to God, through Jesus. Paul says that God wants to be reconciled with every single one of His children.

Do you know that God loves you? Can you hear Him speak words of love over you? Can You hear Him singing His love over you? Zephaniah 3:17 (NLT) says, "For the Lord your God is living among you. He is a mighty savior. He will take delight in you with gladness. With his love, he will calm all your fears. He will rejoice over you with joyful songs." He does. He will. His desire is for more and more relationship with you. God's love and desire is not the problem. Our desire for God is what is lacking.

If we were able to ask Jesus why we find it so difficult to love God, what might His answer be? I believe His first answer would be, "You don't love God, because you don't really know Him." Jesus would tell us that we have not spent enough time in God's presence. We have not spent enough time being with God and talking with God. Jesus often withdrew from the crowds, even from His closest friends, to spend time with God (Luke 5:16).

Is this something that you ever do? Jesus **OFTEN** did. The problem is our lack of desire and lack of availability. May you start every day, every morning, with the awareness of God's desire to spend the day with you and with a desire to spend your day with Him. He loves you. You are His beloved. When you read the designations of love for people in verses like Zechariah 3:17, Ephesians 5:1, and 1 John 4:7, I hope you see yourself in these verses.

Chapter 7 - Discussion Questions

1. What does it mean to you to be God's beloved son or daughter? Why is it hard to believe this truth?

2. What are some ways that your identity as "God's beloved" has been stolen from you?

3. Does the world see people differently than God sees people? Talk about some of the negative ways that people are portrayed in modern books and movies.

4. What are some ways that you are getting to know your Father?

5. Talk about ways that God sings His love and joy over you.

Lovelife

Chapter 8 – How Is Your Lovelife?

If loving God whole-heartedly is the most important goal and activity of your life, then, let me ask you a very important question. How is your love life with God? Do the people around you know that you love God? Can they see it? In this book, I've been using the word, "Lovelife," to describe our life of love for God. I put the two words love and life together and capitalized it (capitalizing it to show that this is something that is connected to God). Your love life, lower caps and two words, can be used to describe your relationship with another person. But, "Lovelife" is the love that you have for God. How is your Lovelife?

"Being in love" is something that is real and easily noticeable. When one of our friends or family members falls in love, it is usually obvious to us, sometimes to the point of the ridiculous. Have you ever been noticed for how much you love God?

Our modern cars are equipped with a number of different devices for measuring some of the different aspects of how our cars are functioning. For instance, cars have a speedometer to tell us how fast we are driving. When a person gets pulled over for speeding, he or she is without excuse because all cars are supposed to have working speedometers. It probably would not help you to try to explain to a police officer that you didn't know how fast you were going because your car did not have a working speedometer. You might get two tickets now! There are other gauges which measure things like gas levels, oil levels, tire pressure and other important aspects of a car being in good running order. If the gas level gauge is ignored, you might find yourself stranded on the side of the road.

What if every Bible, or every person, came equipped with a Lovelife gauge? What if there were a measuring device, like the gas gauge in your car, that could measure the truth and depth of love that you have in your heart for God? I wonder what it would show us about ourselves? I wonder what it would show us about the Lovelives of the people who attend church with us every Sunday?

LOVELIFE

If you are like me, I assume even the thought of such a measuring device makes you a little uneasy in the pit of your stomach. It is easy to put on a false face and go to church. It is easy to put on a new suit or a new dress and go to church. We are skilled at looking good on the outside, while very few people actually know how we are feeling inside.

We all know that everyone goes to church out of love for God. Right? That is not necessarily true. We read our Bibles, go to Sunday school, and say prayers before we eat because we love God. Right? Again, this could be true, but it is not guaranteed. Most of us know that this is not always true in our own lives. Some of us may know that this has never really been true. Some go to church to please parents or grandparents. Some people go to church so people in the community will think better of them or buy insurance from their business. Many go to church and do church things for all the wrong reasons.

So, how is your Lovelife? What would an accurate measuring device really show about how much love you have for God, or worse, would it reveal that you don't have much, if any, love for God? Jesus says the greatest commandment, the most important action for any person, is to be the greatest lover of God that is possible. Jesus says you should love God with your whole being (all your heart, soul, mind, and strength).

Religion can make this effort very confusing, and sometimes something completely different from what was intended by Jesus. Do you love God whole-heartedly? Most people answer this question with answers about going to church, reading the Bible, and doing some good deeds. All those things are fine and good, even biblical, but they say nothing about how much you really love God.

We can usually recognize when a man or woman is truly in love. They talk about their love interest all the time. They notice all the unique and interesting characteristics of the other person. They know many of the likes and dislikes of their special love. They know their lover's favorite foods, favorite books and movies, and favorite color. Lovers pay attention to all the unique aspects of the person that they love.

So how is your Lovelife? What are the things that you appreciate and admire about God? What are His likes and dislikes? What kind of people does God notice and appreciate? What are some of the things that make God happy? What kind of people and actions upset Him? We learn these things about the people that we truly love. When we love God, we will begin to learn many beautiful truths about our Heavenly Father. Our love for Him will grow.

What are some of God's traits that you notice and love? I have made comments like, "God makes the most beautiful sunrises and sunsets!" When I am in the mountains and standing next to a crystal-clear lake or stream, I tell God "Thank You" and I tell Him how much I love Him and His creation.

I am often awestruck when I see a person making the choice to be saved through Jesus, God's plan of salvation. Sometimes when witnessing a baptism, I whisper, "I love you God." Communion is another time where I will express my love for Jesus. Love notices. Love communicates.

If, in reading this chapter, you have made the awful discovery that you may not have ever truly loved God, you are not alone. If you believe that an accurate measuring device of your Lovelife would reveal little or nothing, at least you can know there are many others with the same problem. When Jesus came to earth, this was the reality for most of his immediate family, friends, and for the Jewish family of faith at large. They did not have the love of God in their hearts.

In the first five chapters of the Gospel of John, Jesus reveals Himself to the people of His day. John 1:10-11 contains some sobering and sad verses. John says, "He (Jesus) was in the world, and though the world was made through him, the world did not recognize him. He came to that which was his own, but his own did not receive him." Jesus was not loved and accepted by the very people that He created. John 1:3 says that Jesus created the whole world and all the people in the world. By John 5:18, the people not only don't love and accept Jesus, but they already are very determined to kill Him. How was that possible? How did Jesus, the Son of God, come to His own creation and find that very few of His created children loved or accepted Him?

Jesus told them what their problem was in John 5:42. He explained to them that they were much more concerned about the praise of their fellow man, than the love and praise of God. He said very tragically, "…I know you. I know that you do not have the love of God in your hearts." The people of Israel, the children of Abraham (who was a friend and lover of Almighty God), did not love God. They had no Lovelife! They were religious in every way. They were religious in ways that were considered fanatical by the rest of the world. Jesus said that they looked good and faithful, but there was no (none, zip, zero) love for God in their hearts.

LOVELIFE

I am going to assume that you are reading this book because you want to love God more. You want to have a rich Lovelife with God. Let me tell you something exciting and meaningful as you move into this endeavor. **He is worthy of all your love!** He is beautiful enough, awesome enough, and good enough to deserve your love for a lifetime and for all of eternity. Everything the Father says and does is worthy of your love and worship. If you knew everything that God was doing at this exact moment, that understanding alone could fill a lifetime with worship and love. The more you know about Him, the more that you will love Him.

One of the HUGE difficulties in loving God, for most people, is that they do not believe that He is loveable. All the lies of Hell come against God's beauty, goodness, and character. We all have places where we have agreed with the lies of the enemy, especially when it comes to God. People describe God as unavailable, uncaring, unloving. They believe that He is vindictive and mean. They believe that God wants most people to go to hell. Jesus did not talk about God that way. So, how many false beliefs about God have you accepted?

Jesus was very clear about His love for his Father (John 14:31). Jesus described God as a good father. Jesus said that

He is a better Father than any earthly father, or grandfather. Jesus would tell you that God loves you more than your mother or grandmother. Really. God is a Father that never stops waiting for the return of His lost and hurting children. He never stops loving His children. He wants all of them to return to His love and live in loving relationship with Him. Jesus is the only person that lived in the fullness of that relationship.

Jesus said that God is worthy of all the love that your heart can summon. Your Heavenly Father is worth all your love and adoration because everything He does is good and loving. God is worthy of the worship of your whole body. God is so awesome and beautiful and lovely that you and I can learn to love Him with our whole being, in every part our lives. To make this your daily effort, the goal of your daily life, is the most important effort that you can make!!!

How is your Lovelife? How do you start to improve your Lovelife? The important thing is that you start. Now. Today. God is totally worthy of all your love.

LOVELIFE

Chapter 8 – Discussion Questions

1. How is your Lovelife with the Father? If a gauge could really test your love for God, what would it show?

2. Has religion turned "loving God" into something else in your life? Do you claim to love God but have no real evidence that can be seen or measured?

3. What are some of the things that you notice and appreciate (love) about God?

4. What are some things that you love about God's heart? How does God reveal His good heart to you each day?

5. Have you made your Lovelife a daily priority? Talk about your answer.

Lovelife

Chapter 9 – False Lovers

The devil knows scripture. He quotes scripture to Jesus, during Jesus' 40 days of fasting and temptation, to try and get Him to sin. So, we should assume that the devil knows that the first and greatest commandment is to love God with our whole being. Since the devil knows that this is the most important goal and activity that a human can be engaged in, then it makes sense, that a top priority of the enemy is ***to stop us from loving God***. The devil does not want anyone to love God. When it comes to distracting us from a Lovelife with God, what does he do? **ANYTHING!** The devil will do anything to keep us from loving God with our whole hearts, or with any part of our selves.

The enemy loves to lie about God's love for you and me. This is why in John 8:44, Jesus calls the devil the father of all lies. The enemy likes to tell us that while God may love some heroes of the faith, that you and I are not included in that list. Along with listening to the lies, we simply give the enemy easy places to attack because of our own sin and rebellion. Each of us has struggles and sins that are common to all mankind, but we each have some that are specifically unique to us. The enemy likes to tell us that we are alone in our sins and that to confess them to another person would be very damaging to us. I have believed that lie most of my life. Therefore, I kept my deepest struggles hidden from others for many years. Sadly, to make things worse, I could play the part of "Mr. Good Guy Christian" well. But the enemy would remind me at significant times that God knew "everything" and was not pleased. God was not pleased with my sin (which is true), but he was really not pleased with me, as His son (NOT true). That was and is a lie from the enemy I still have to renounce regularly.

Here is a question that I want you to try to answer about yourself. How many lies of the enemy are you currently living under? Maybe they are partial truths, but still a lie. How many things do you believe about yourself, others, or God Himself that are simply not true? Many have never considered this question. When the question first hit home to me, I was stunned at how many lies were currently in place and working damage in my life. It was painful to know how long they had been there and to remember the times and places, many years before, where I had accepted these lies as truths in my life. The man that was sharing this idea with me wanted me to identify one or two lies that were a part of my life. I quickly saw that there was not just one to two, but there were many. There were so many lies that it reminded me of the story of Legion, in Mark 5:9. I had to write the lies down and then renounce them, one by one, in the name of Jesus.

Here was one of my false beliefs that I didn't know about until I specifically looked for lies in my life. The lie was, "I am a bad speaker with very little of importance to say." I really believed that I was not saying anything helpful or important. I believed people did not want to listen to my words for many valid reasons. Can you imagine what a devastating belief that was for a preacher? That was my job at the time! This lie, and many more, were revealed to me by the Spirit. I renounced them all in the name of Jesus Christ. I said out loud, "I renounce in Jesus's name that I am a bad speaker with nothing to say." One by one, I went down the list of lies that I had written, and then, renounced each one in Jesus' name. One of the biggest lies that I renounced was that God did not like me, and therefore, could never really love me.

The next week when I preached a sermon, two of the leaders in the local church came up to me and asked me what had happened. What had caused the changes they saw and heard? I told them that I had come out from under a "legion" of lies in my life. They acknowledged that they could see and hear the difference.

So, how many lies are currently at work in your life? The enemy lies about our value as people, our giftedness, our friendships, and what other people think about us. The enemy lies about these kinds of things, and more, all the time. If we are vulnerable to one lie or many lies, he uses it (or them) against us in every significant situation of our lives. He steals, kills, and destroys with his lies (John 10:10). So, how many do you have? Make a list. Renounce each one in the name of Jesus. Begin to walk in truth and freedom.

Here is a good place to start. Do you believe that you are a one-of-a-kind beloved child of your Heavenly Father? A lot of Christians know those words as a fact from scripture. They know the truth of the statement, but don't believe the words apply to them. Do you accept and feel deep in your heart that God loves you? Do you know that He loves you with a greater love than any other person in your life?

LOVELIFE

If God's love is hard for you to accept personally, you are under lies of the enemy. The enemy is stealing and destroying the life that God wants for you. Ask God to reveal the lies. Ask Him to show you the origins of the lies. There are lies from the enemy, from people, from the world, and from your own failures and mistakes. They might be based on true events, but they are still just a lie. Partial truths are still a lie. Ask God to reveal them, and then, you need to renounce each one in the name of Jesus. This is part of the process of 2 Corinthians 10:5. Paul says we are to capture our thoughts and make them obedient to the truth of Jesus.

The enemy also tries to keep us distracted with false loves and lovers. There are distractions like money, sex, power, food, and fame. Those are some of the things that many in the world are going after to make their lives better. Paul says, in Romans 1:25, that the people of the world have "exchanged the truth of God for a lie, and worshiped and served created things rather than the Creator..." They do not understand that false gods (along with the lies of the enemy) will never deliver on any of their promises. In fact, false gods will always steal the very things they promise to give to you. Sex addicts end up alone. Caffeine and nicotine addicts end up being more nervous. Drug and alcohol addicts, who want to escape the burdens of life for a while, find that they cannot escape their addictions.

Sex, as a gift from God, draws us into relationship with our spouses. Sex, as a false god, leads towards isolation and loneliness and the belief that a real, meaningful (the "naked and unashamed" of Genesis 2:25) relationship is not possible. God is better than sex. God is better than money. God is better than chocolate. God is better than any false god. False gods keep us from a healthy loving relationship with our Heavenly Father. One of the truths of scripture (Matthew 6:24) is that no one can serve two masters, or two gods. It is impossible to be in a loving relationship with God, while desperately clinging to a false god. God refers to this as adultery in James 4:4. We are adulterous lovers when we claim to love God but still cling to our "other lovers" and false gods.

For those of you who are married, think about what your spouse would think about the following example. Let's say you are a man and you are married. What would your wife say to you if you came to her and told her that you love her very much, but you were going to be having a few extra relationships on the side? You tell her, "I love you and I want to stay married to you, but sometimes I'll be spending the night with other women. You will be my number one wife and they will be secondary wives or lovers." Would your wife go for that arrangement? Would your husband accept your unfaithfulness if the situation were reversed?

This is the way that God thinks about your relationship with Him. He wants you for Himself alone. James 4:5 (NCV) says, "Do you think the scripture means nothing that says, "The Spirit that God made to live in us wants us for himself alone?"" God loves you so much that He doesn't want you to have any false lovers in your life. He knows that they are liars. He knows that they will hurt you and me. The beautiful part of this, a part that is so easily missed, is how much God loves you and desires an intimate relationship with you. Remember the oft repeated words of the Old Testament, "God is good and His love endures forever." He desires our love and we desperately need His.

God never lies. He doesn't deceive us into loving Him in order to use and hurt us. That is what the enemy does. Bring every lie into the light of Jesus. Identify and get rid of the false lovers. Pour out your love on God!

There are countless distractions of the enemy. So, let me ask you the question one more time. How many of these lies, false lovers, false gods, are in your life? Some of these things may have been in your life for years. The enemy fed you lies and offered you substitute gods at vulnerable times in your life. Many of these came when you were young and naïve. Ask God to reveal the lies, false gods, and any false lovers that are in your life. Renounce the lies. Renounce the false lovers. Renounce the false gods. You can't serve a false god and love your Heavenly Father at the same time. The most important command for our lives is to love God with our whole and undivided heart. How is your Lovelife?

Chapter 9 - Discussion Questions

1. What are some reasons that the enemy tries to keep us from loving God? What is the enemy scared of, and more accurately, what does he hate?

2. Have you ever struggled with the idea that God doesn't like you very much? When did you start to have this belief in your life?

3. How many lies of the enemy are currently at work in your life? Are there a few or are there many? Have you ever brought them into the light of Jesus and renounced everything that does not stand up to His Truth?

4. Do you recognize some false gods and false lovers in your life? Name them. Then, renounce them out loud with a trusted Christian friend.

5. What difference would it make in your life to be free from the lies of the enemy?

Lovelife

Chapter 10 – Falling In Love With Jesus

Colossians 1:15-20:
"He is the image of the invisible God, the firstborn over all creation. For by him all things were created: things in heaven and on earth, visible and invisible, whether thrones or powers or rulers or authorities; all things were created by him and for him. He is before all things, and in him all things hold together. And he is the head of the body, the church; he is the beginning and the firstborn from among the dead, so that in everything he might have the supremacy. For God was pleased to have all his fullness dwell in him, and through him to reconcile to himself all things, whether things on earth or things in heaven, by making peace through his blood, shed on the cross."

Have you ever been in love? Do you remember how the process of "falling in love" happened? It is part indescribable mystery and other part very focused and intentional effort.

Where does love with another person begin? It starts with an encounter. Whether the encounter is intentional or seemingly accidental, two people meet and then begin to have a relationship together. The exact way that this happens is different for every relationship. Some relationships never get beyond a mere acquaintance. But some relationships turn into more, and some into much more. We have people we know by sight but know nothing else about their lives. We know some people through some small, brief interactions, but the relationship with them never turns into anything more. These are our acquaintances.

Next, we have people that we call our friends. These are the people that we like. These are the people with whom we form attachments and to whom we make greater commitments of time and energy. They often are involved in our lives in bigger ways. These are the people that we see often and enjoy the times that we are together. This is a smaller group of people. There is a larger amount of people that are acquaintances, but just a few that become friends.

Then we have those people in life that we call close friends or best friends. These people know many things about us and share many of our likes and dislikes. Most people have only a few really close friends. We keep up with these people even after we are separated by time and space. These are our friends for life.

But then there are the deepest categories of relationship and friendship. These are the people that we love. These are the friends that are a part of our lives, no matter what. These are the members of our family. For most people, the greatest love of life is the person that they decide to marry. This is the one with whom they share possessions and living spaces, have children, and call family, and vow *till death do us part*. Our closest loved ones know the intimate details of our lives and we know most of the details of their lives.

God wants to be the highest level of friendship, relationship, and love that is possible for us to have. The first and greatest commandment in the Bible is that we are to love God with our whole hearts and every part of our being. We are to love God with everything we have and every part of who we are. We are to love Him first and foremost, more than anybody else or anything else. God desires that there should be nothing or no person more important than Him in our lives.

So how do we learn to love God in this way? The answer is that loving God has to begin like any other relationship in our lives. He will start off as an acquaintance and then move to a casual friend. If we stay committed to the relationship, then

God can become a close friend and eventually someone that we truly love. God wants to be loved by us whole-heartedly. He wants to be the greatest love of our lives.

Does this seem possible to you? Does it seem possible to have a full-hearted, lifelong, loving relationship with the God who created the universe, your Father in heaven? Where are you in the process of developing this kind of relationship with God?

For me, figuring out how to love God always seemed like a difficult, if not impossible, endeavor. I felt like God was invisible, untouchable, and too far away. Can I offer a suggestion that helped me? Start by learning to love Jesus. Jesus is Immanuel – God with us.

Jesus gives God a form that we can understand and a humanity to which we can relate. Learn to love Jesus. I began a greater depth of relationship with Jesus during a time of growth in my personal spiritual life. I was in college and spent two summers working for a Christian camp, where I took care of 10-15 junior high boys, every day for three months. We talked about the Bible and our faith every day. They would end up asking me lots of personal questions about me and my faith. They especially wanted to know about the ways that I had struggled and failed in my teenage years. I did not like exposing myself as a very faulty human role model. I learned to direct them away from me and towards Jesus. He is the model. He is the goal. He is the example. To be a Christian is to be a follower of Jesus. I wanted these young people to follow Jesus and not follow in the mistakes of my life.

At this same time, there was a minister at the church I attended in my first years of college that began to teach me how to be a lover of Jesus. I began to read the New Testament gospels. I read Max Lucado books about Jesus. I went to a different college to learn more about the Bible and to grow deeper in my faith. Over the next years I began to discover Jesus to be the most amazing, awesome, fearless, powerful, beautiful, wise, and loving person I had ever heard about or known.

For the next years of my life, I knew that I loved Jesus, but still didn't know what to do with God. It took me many more years to understand that to love Jesus was to love God. Jesus says very simply in John 12:45 (also John 14:9: and Paul, in Col. 1:15) that to see Him is the same as seeing God. Jesus and God are inseparably connected. It would take me many more years to begin to learn how to include the Holy Spirit into the equation.

LOVELIFE

I learned to love Jesus. Beginning with Jesus, I have learned that I love God. I have learned to appreciate and love the Holy Spirit. I wrote a short song years ago that expresses some of this:

> Good morning loving Father,
> Good morning joyful Savior,
> Good morning peaceful Spirit,
> You're here with me today.
> I love you Father,
> I love you Savior,
> I love you Spirit,
> I'll walk with You today.
> I love you Jesus, you're here with me today.

If you are having trouble figuring out how to love God, or the Holy Spirit, then just start with Jesus. He was a human being like you and me. He had a life to which we can relate. He dealt with life, pain, death, and other people in ways that we can understand and appreciate. Learn to love Jesus. Fall in love with Him. The rest comes much easier when there is a good starting place. Jesus, himself, recommends this approach to his followers.

In John 14, the apostles were beginning to understand that something was going to happen to Jesus. He told them not to worry because he was going to his Father's house to prepare a place for them. Thomas told Jesus that they didn't understand what he was talking about, much less how to get there. Jesus told them in John 14:6, that He is the way, the truth, and the life. Jesus is the way to get to the Father. Jesus is the way to know the Father. Those words are still true for us today. Jesus is the way!

Later in John 14, Philip asked Jesus to show them the Father. In John 14:9, Jesus tells Philip and the other apostles that seeing Him, Jesus, is the same as seeing the Father. Start with Jesus. According to the Apostle Peter, in 1 Peter 1:20-21, Jesus is a great starting place to grow faith in God. Peter says that through Jesus people can believe in God. When you and I love Jesus, we are loving God.

So, examine the life of Jesus. Look at the way He lived. Look at the way He treated people and the things He did for His Father. Look at the fearless and faithful way that He died. Jesus lived a life that is worthy of our appreciation and devotion. He awakens our love because of His demonstrated love for us on the cross. He awakens our love for God because of the way He loved God. Jesus is a friend who can be with you throughout every day. Jesus is a person who has had to deal with all the struggles of humanity and life. He has dealt with frustration and anger. He dealt with physical and sexual temptations (Hebrews 4:15). He was like us in every way. His ability to love and forgive people is awe-inspiring. Fall in love with Jesus. When you love Jesus, you are loving God. When you appreciate Jesus' heart, you are appreciating God's heart. Start there.

Chapter 10 - Discussion Questions

1. Talk about some of the differences in relationship between your acquaintances and your friends.

2. Now talk about some of the differences between friends and those that you claim to love.

3. According to Jesus, God is supposed to be your best friend and highest love. What are some reasons that this seems hard?

4. What do you think of the idea of learning to love God by learning to love Jesus?

5. Read 1 Peter 1:20 -21. What do you think of Peter's statement in verse 21 that "through Jesus you believe in God?" What do you think he means?

LOVELIFE

Chapter 11 – Learning To Love

To love God with everything that you are is the greatest commandment in the Bible. But how do you learn to love God? How do you practice? Here are a few more practical suggestions.

Read God's Word

To fall in love with God demands that you learn to spend time with God. You must get to know God better. Getting to know God better always begins with God's written word, the Bible. God reveals His heart and His truth in the words of the Bible. The more familiar that you are with God's word, the more opportunity you have to develop a real relationship with God.

How many Christians have never read the Bible? At this time in history, there is really no excuse. There are numerous, understandable, and very carefully translated versions of the Bible out there. Choose one and start reading. Download a modern, easy to understand, version of the Bible on your phone, tablet, or computer and start reading. Read it! One of the first ways that the enemy attacks our desire to grow in relationship with God is by making this task seem too hard.

The Bible is NOT too hard to read and understand. It is meant to be read. It would be tragic to find how many ways an older version of the Bible, like the King James, has made Bible reading too difficult for modern God seekers. There is often legalism and fear attached to reading any version other than the King James. This has kept many from reading and learning and growing in relationship with God. The Bible was meant to be read and understood. Begin today. Start with the New Testament. Start with Luke and Acts and then read the rest. You can go back and read the other 3 gospels later. It takes about the same amount of time as reading a paperback novel. Some of you read a novel every few days.

Next, read the whole Bible through in a year. If that moves too slowly, read the whole Bible in a few months. There are many easy to follow Bible reading plans available. Read the Bible. Learn. Grow in your love and appreciation for God.

<u>Talk to God</u>

How much time do you spend talking with God? Just the "churchy" religious idea of how people should pray keeps many from praying. Paul says in 1 Thess. 5, that we should pray continually. Other versions say that we should pray without ceasing. We can and should pray all the time. We should have a continual line of communication open between us and God, between us and Jesus. We should be learning to talk with God throughout each and every day.

But many of us still don't pray. And when we pray, it is often not heartfelt and truthful communication with God. If we talked to a spouse or family member the same way we prayed to God, they would ask us what kind of weird game that we were playing. There are times, like a church service, where we pray in a specific way that is appropriate to that time and that situation. But most of the time, when we are praying to God, it should sound more like an intimate conversation with a good friend or a loved family member. It should be real. We should talk about the things that matter to us and the things presently happening in our lives.

God wants us to love Him more than anything or anyone else. That can't be faked. Our most intimate friends and family would not tolerate us talking to them or babbling at them, without really saying or meaning anything. Real love communicates. Love goes out of its way to communicate in personal and meaningful ways with the beloved.

Learning to talk with God, throughout every moment of our lives, changes everything. You are going to discover that not only are you free to talk with God about anything, but He really wants you to talk to Him about everything. What's even better, is you are going to begin to hear Him talking back. Relationship, especially intimate loving relationship, is always a two-way street.

If you have grown up in American churches, there is a good chance that you have heard the song, "In the Garden," by Charles Austin Miles. It describes a deep level of relationship between a follower and Jesus, or describes what Jesus experienced when he would ***often*** (Luke 5:16) go off by himself and pray. The chorus says:

> "And He walks with me, and He talks with me,
> And He tells me I am His own,
> And the joy we share as we tarry there,
> None other has ever known."[1]

God is after that kind of relationship with each of his beloved children, with each of us. So, how do you begin to cultivate this depth of relationship with God?

<u>Make Time For God</u>

How do you find the time to spend with God? In order to find time, you are going to have to make time! I know for sure that it will not happen unless you are very intentional about cutting out a space for focused prayer. Once again, the enemy will do anything and everything to disrupt this effort.

I have learned to turn off the radio when I am driving and spend those minutes and hours talking to God. I begin by looking around and noticing anything for which I can thank God. I have "discovered" beautiful flowers (some of them are beautiful blooming weeds!), incredible birds, exquisite butterflies and awesome lakes, vistas, sunrises and sunsets. It is amazing how many things don't get noticed because we don't take the time to look. And even when we look, we don't remember to thank God, who is the creator of all that is good and beautiful. We need to learn to express our thanksgiving to Him with words of love.

For two years, in my desire to spend time with God, I made it a practice to journal something I was learning about God every day. Sometimes I would talk about things I had seen or learned. Sometimes I would journal about something that I thought God might be trying to tell me. Listening to God has seemed impossible to me, most of my life. But, amazingly, when I go back over the two years of daily journal entries, it is obvious that real and important conversations were taking place. Important matters were being discussed and real learning was taking place.

I have also set aside the time to go on both formal and informal retreats, where the whole reason for going was to find God and hear "anything" from God. It worked there and can work anywhere else! God wants to be found and heard!

One of my first efforts to get away to talk and listen to God felt like a total failure at the time. I went out to a secluded camping spot and spent two days in fasting and prayer. A friendly neighbor kept inviting me to eat steak and share meals with his family. I came back with poison ivy from my head to my toes! I was frustrated and angry over this failed experiment. The poison ivy burned and itched for two months.

Over the following years, I began to realize in how many ways that "poison ivy filled" weekend was a beautiful success. It was obviously opposed by the enemy, but for me, it was a turning point and an important beginning of finding desperately needed time with God. I read through most of the New Testament in those two days because I didn't believe I could hear Him speaking. Remember, reading the New Testament takes about the same amount of time as reading a novel. Reading the Bible is never a waste of time! As it turns out, God was doing much more speaking and communicating than I understood or gave Him credit for at that time.

Don't forget that if talking to God seems too hard, talk to Jesus. Jesus knows what it is like to walk in our shoes. He really wore shoes! Jesus knows what pain and suffering feels like. Jesus knows about dust, sweat, bugs, and poison plants. Jesus knows, and Jesus is God. He is Immanuel, God with us. The Spirit is God in us. Ask the Spirit for help. Speak to God. Find time to speak with Him often. Get away, if you need to, to find focused time to spend with God. Be ready for opposition and distraction from the enemy. The important thing is to begin. It will change everything! He will change everything. It is the way we begin to live out the greatest commandment. Relationship with us is God's great desire. Relationship with God is our greatest need.

Chapter 11 - Discussion Questions

1. Have you ever tried to read through the Bible? How did you do? What was good? What was hard?

2. Discuss some of the issues with reading different versions of the Bible. Talk about which version you use and some reasons it has worked for you.

3. Do you have a prayer life? Would you say that your prayers are real and meaningful? Have there been times that you have prayed without really talking with God?

4. What does it mean to "pray without ceasing?" Is this possible in our daily lives? What might it look like for you to live in constant relationship and communication with God?

5. Journaling can be a good way to focus your thoughts on God. Record the things you believe He is saying to you through His Spirit, in your heart. Share some examples where you believe God has communicated with you?

Chapter 12 – Words of Love

How do you talk to a person that you love? Do you speak to them differently than someone who is an acquaintance? We usually try to tell the people that we love, "I love you." And we don't just tell them once. We tell them often, and we show them in many different ways that we mean what we say.

One of the difficulties about having a Lovelife with God is that it seems especially strange to tell Him, "I love you." We often don't remember to tell Him, "Thank you" for the all the things that we have asked Him to give us, much less tell Him that we love Him. Sometimes it is hard to believe that God desires to hear these kinds of expressions of love and appreciation from us.

I believe that this is essential to developing a full-hearted loving relationship with God. We need to tell Him many times a day "Thank you," and "I love you." Maybe you could try that right now. "Father, I love you." That wasn't too hard. Now, you need to get better at expressing your love. If loving God is the most important command, then, it would follow that verbal expressions of love for God are important words to learn to speak.

When you see a beautiful sunrise or sunset. Don't just appreciate them silently. Tell God, the creator of all sunrises and sunsets, thank you. Express your love and appreciation to Him for all the beauty of His creation. In that moment, tell God "I love you." If you and I like to be told that we are loved and appreciated, then why should it seem strange that God, in whose image we were created, would want to frequently hear our expressions of love for Him? God desires to be recognized, appreciated, and loved.

When you realize in moments of clarity some of the awful trials that Jesus had to endure on the cross, don't just check it off as something learned and move on. Express your love and thankfulness. "Jesus, I love you so much. Thank you for enduring the shame and suffering that really should have been my shame and suffering. I really do love you. You are beautiful and amazing. You have been so good to me!"

Sometimes the Holy Spirit will show us things or tell us things that we desperately need at a specific time. Sometimes

He will reveal His heart in a beautiful and powerful way. This happens in worship or when reading the Bible and suddenly the words and the story go deeper because we get a glimpse, or a clearer picture, of God's goodness and love. Tell Him "thank you" and "I love you" and "I really appreciate your heart."

Do you see how moments of recognition could break forth into expressions of love and thankfulness and praise? How would our worship services and our personal times of fellowship with God be different if we were actually caught up in overwhelming wonder, love, and thankfulness to Jesus and learning to express that love with our whole being? We would worship Him with more of our hearts and minds. We would love Him and worship Him more fully. We would be living out the first and greatest commandment!

Have you ever tried to write a letter or a poem to somebody that you love? This is where many of the songs that we sing originated. The children of God tried to put down in words their love and worship for the Father, for Jesus, for the Holy Spirit, for God. When I started trying to journal, it often felt difficult and random at the time I was writing. But now that I have been doing this for years, it is amazing to read things that I wrote down many years ago. I often don't remember the difficulties of those far away times, but the words are encouraging to me in what I am going through today. Sometimes, I put my thoughts into poetry, just because they are hard to write down any other way. I wrote this poem in one of my journals over 20 years ago, when I was reading through the Bible looking for more of God. I had just finished reading Psalm 127 and wrote the following:

> Don't trust in the skills of a builder,
> To protect what is precious to you,
> But look to the love of the Father,
> His love is faithful and true.
>
> Chorus
> Peace and rest are found in Him,
> Look to God above,
> For safety and security,
> For sleep to those He loves.
>
> Don't trust in the power of an army,
> To secure the borders of your land,
> But trust in the power of the Father,
> To save you with His almighty hand.
>
> Chorus
>
> In vain you rise up early,
> In vain you stay up late,
> By yourself you can do nothing,
> To fill your broken, empty plate.
>
> Chorus

LOVELIFE

I don't remember when I wrote this poem or why I wrote it. I wrote the words, but never put it to music. Most importantly, the thoughts are good, beautiful, and speak to a growing relationship of love for God.

Another time, a few years later, I was in between jobs and praying earnestly that God would take care of me and my new wife. We were hoping to start a family and looking for the ability and the direction of where to go and what to do. Have you been there? There are many times we get frustrated, or depressed, and spend months, maybe even years, wandering hopelessly in the desert. At one such time in my life, I decided to begin journaling out of sheer desperation to hear "anything" from God. My belief at the time was that I was not hearing anything from God. I certainly was not getting any job opportunities or leads. I wrote the following poem right in the middle of journal entries that were expressing my frustrations:

> To trust that God is directing each step,
> Even when I think that I am lost.
> To praise God for every situation in life,
> Even when I feel that I have been deserted.
> To NOT pull away from God
> In my thoughts and prayers,
> Even when I think He has pulled away from me.
> To accept that I am loved and cherished,
> Even when I feel ugly and weak.
> To decide to smile, laugh, and live joyously,

LOVELIFE

Even when it seems that God doesn't care.
This is faith. This is rest. This is peace.

I put a title on that journal of 20 years ago, "Learning to Walk with God." It could just as easily have been titled "Learning to love God."

By the way, I didn't come up with these forms of expression on my own. The Bible is full of songs, poems, and expressions of love to God. Many of the psalms of David are examples of his efforts to love and worship God in the middle of difficult times. He wrote songs and poems to God all his life. Read Psalms 36 and 63.

Moses, Miriam, Solomon, the prophets, Matthew, Mark, Luke, John, Paul, Peter, James, and Jude all found ways of expressing their love and appreciation to God. They wrote some very beautiful, powerful, and inspired words to guide our hearts and minds in our love for God. How is your Lovelife? Are you learning to express your love with your words?

Since those first beginnings, I have filled up numerous journals with hundreds of entries and my goal has not changed. I want to walk with God (Father, Son, and Spirit), and learn to love and appreciate Him each and every day. This world is infinitely full of God's creation and offers infinite possibilities to tell God "Thank you" and "I love you Father." How is your

LOVELIFE

Lovelife? Are you growing in relationship, appreciation, admiration, and love? Jesus says that this is the most important thing that anybody can do!

When I read the Bible, especially the stories about Jesus, I have learned to tell Jesus "I love you" right in the middle of my reading. Jesus loved people and had compassion on people in ways that I cannot yet accomplish. Jesus was faithful and trusting in places where I would have quickly quit and given up. I really do love and appreciate Jesus. He is amazing! He is awesome! He is the person that I most want to emulate in my life. He is my hero. And I know that Jesus said that He was only doing what God, the Father, has always been doing (John 5:19). I love and appreciate the heart of my heavenly Father. I try to tell God I love Him every day, the same way that I tell my wife and kids each day. Jesus tells us that God deserves more of our love than anybody or anything else. Tell Him. Sing to Him. Write to Him. Express your love. It changes everything!

There is not a right or wrong way to do any of these things. The key is to begin. Lack of desire for relationship has never been God's problem but has always been our problem. Start the relationship. Begin loving God. This relationship has infinite room for growth and expression, because it is a relationship with your Infinite Father. Make yourself available. God is always available.

Chapter 12 - Discussion Questions

1. How many times have you told your spouse and kids you love them? How many times have you told God, or Jesus, or the Spirit? Discuss your answers.

2. Talk about your prayer life. How many of your prayers are requests to God? How many are expressions of thankfulness and love?

3. Have you ever told Jesus, in prayer, how much you love Him for what He did on the cross? Why or why not?

4. Have you ever written a poem or song to God? What did you talk about or what would you want to talk about?

5. How was David able to write so many psalms to God? What are some things these poems and songs reveal about David's relationship with God?

Lovelife

Chapter 13 – Worship

"With my body, I thee worship…"
Anglican Book of Common Prayer

One of the greatest proofs of a growing Lovelife with God is a thriving life of worship. Love and worship are intertwined, as the words from the old English wedding ceremony so beautifully articulate. True love breaks forth into worship. People worship those things and people that they love. They can't help but speak words of worship and praise. They can't help but demonstrate with all of themselves the depth of love and appreciation they have for their beloved.

When a young man starts to love a sport, he will often proclaim his love. "I love football!" "I love being able to watch a game and see my favorite players!" As love for the sport grows, so does the depth of understanding, along with ever increasing words of worship and appreciation for all the different aspects of the game. There is a growing passion for the game. He wants to constantly be out practicing and playing with others. Great players learn the plays and are constantly thinking about ways to improve themselves and their team. The best players are the strongest and most physically prepared to endure not only a game, but a whole season of games.

Jesus says we are supposed to love God with all our heart, soul, mind, and strength. I want to talk briefly about each of those categories and how to begin to love and worship God with each. This is not an exhaustive chapter on how to do these things, but a bare bones introduction. You will have to find your own personal expressions of love and worship in each of these areas. A healthy worship life is one of the greatest indicators of a growing and healthy Lovelife with God.

Heart

Who are the people and what are the things that you love most in life? We are full of passion for the things that we love to do. Do you greatly desire more relationship with God? Are you passionate about God? What do you love about Him? What are the characteristics about Jesus that move you to tears?

I sometimes try to picture what the experience of meeting the gaze of Jesus would be like. His eyes had to speak powerfully about all that was in His heart. I, personally, can't wait to see Him. I believe that His eyes will communicate the love and acceptance that I have hungered for all my life.

Jesus physically touched people that no one else in His culture would touch. Jesus touched lepers. Jesus touched sinful women. His touch was always appropriate and desperately needed. There are songs that have been written about Jesus' touch alone. There are so many characteristics about Jesus that win the love of our hearts. In fact, no other love from any other source other than God is big enough to capture the depths of your heart. God is awesome enough and beautiful enough to capture more and more of your heart each moment, for the rest of eternity. May you and I learn to love and worship God with all our hearts.

Soul

One way to summarize the soul is that it is everything about us that is unique and eternal. Your soul is the essence of who you are. Your soul is not limited by your physical body. When the body dies, the soul goes somewhere else. The soul was created for eternity.

LOVELIFE

One of the great disappointments of life is the way that everything breaks, and everybody gets sick and dies. We have a deep longing for life to be beautiful and meaningful and everlasting. The reality is, sooner or later, we lose everything and everyone. It is frustrating and feels, in the words of the writer of Ecclesiastes, meaningless.

One of the things that I love about God is His desire to restore the hope that all the good and beautiful and meaningful parts of life can be enjoyed for eternity (1 Peter 5:10). It is the hope of heaven. Jesus promised his disciples, in John 14, that He was going to prepare a place for them in His Father's kingdom. He promised that the life for which they all hope and long for was going to be a reality someday. It was the opportunity Jesus came to give to any who would seek the Father and His Kingdom. Jesus is the way to this everlasting life that we seek.

With God, there is so much more that awaits us in eternity. There is always more. There is a better quality and quantity of life available. Finally, the day will come when we will get to enjoy all that for which we were created. I love Jesus for his offer of life! I love Jesus and the provision He has made for you and me. One day, we will receive the fullness of life that we so long for now. What are some ways you are learning to love and worship God with your eternal soul?

Mind

What captivates your thinking these days? Who are the people and what are the things that activate and energize your mind? One of the significant ways that we were created to love and worship God is with our minds. In Romans 12:2, Paul says that Christians are to be transformed, completely renewed, in their minds.

God belongs in our deepest thoughts and studies. The mathematical precision of our world and universe is incredible! Our earth must be the exact right distance from the sun for our earth, and everything on it, to survive. The precision that is found in God's creation is stunning. God's glory is worthy of our love and adoration.

Humans have the incredible ability to think and reason through all kinds of issues and problems. There are people who have spent a lifetime studying and learning about some minute piece of life. Think about doctors who have learned to do brain surgery. Think about scientists who have given their lives to study one species of animal life or plant life.

We can learn to love and appreciate God in all our thinking. Paul says in Philippians 4:8 that we are to discipline our minds to think about things that are true, noble, right, pure, lovely, admirable, excellent and praiseworthy. These are the kinds of things that Christians are to think about. These are the kinds of things that come from God and deserve our worship. Are you learning to love and worship God with your mind?

<u>Strength</u>

We all live with an awareness of incredible power that is all around us. We feel it in the strength of our muscles and other physical abilities. There is also the power that is all around us in in nature and in the world. What is there about God's power that you are learning to love? When you accomplish some physical feat, with your human strength, it should give you another reason to worship God. Jesus says we are to love God and worship God with our strength.

David worshipped God and danced before Him with all his might. Elijah got caught up in the power of God and ran with all his strength. Samson displayed the power of God, when the Spirit of God would come upon him, and he would perform incredible feats of strength to the glory of God. Jesus had a strength of character that still challenges the hearts of all His followers. There are many examples in the Bible of people serving God with the strength that God has given them.

Have you ever been awed by a powerful "act of God" out in nature? Have you been caught outside in the middle of a thunderstorm? Even more awesome, have you ever been caught out on a lake in the middle of a thunderstorm? The apostles experienced the frightening power of the storm, but then found themselves worshipping the more awesome power of Jesus. What are the ways that you are learning to love and worship God with all your strength?

Conclusion

Have you heard the saying, "imitation is the greatest form of flattery?" We worship and emulate heroes in many different areas of life. Sometimes we call this hero worship. We talk constantly about the people we love and admire. We praise them for all their abilities to create and excel beyond others. We talk about all their great deeds. Have you fallen in love with Jesus this way? Do you love Him and desire to be more like Him? What are the characteristics of God that make you love Him and make you want to worship Him? Love and worship go hand in hand.

LOVELIFE

Chapter 13 – Discussion Questions

1. Talk about ways that love and worship are connected.

2. What are some characteristics about God's heart that you love?

3. What are some characteristics of God's eternal nature, and your eternal soul, that you appreciate?

4. What are some characteristics of God that you find worthy of worship with your mind?

5. What are some characteristics of God's power and your own physical strength that are awesome to you?

Chapter 14 – An Important Last Word

Remember where we started in Mark 12:28-31:

"One of the teachers of the law came and heard them debating. Noticing that Jesus had given them a good answer, he asked him, "Of all the commandments, which is the most important?" "The most important one," answered Jesus, "is this: 'Hear, O Israel, the Lord our God, the Lord is one. Love the Lord your God with all your heart and with all your soul and with all your mind and with all your strength.' The second is this: 'Love your neighbor as yourself.' There is no commandment greater than these."

The most important command is to love God with our whole being. The second greatest commandment is to love your neighbor as you love yourself.

One of the best ways to determine how you are doing in your Lovelife is to explore how you are currently loving people. The Apostle John says in 1 John 4:20-21, "If anyone says, "I love God," yet hates his brother, he is a liar. For anyone who does not love his brother, whom he has seen, cannot love God, who he has not seen. And he has given us this command: Whoever loves God must also love his brother." How are you doing loving people?

As you grow in your Lovelife with God, you are supposed to begin to realize how undeserving, but blessed, you are to be in God's love. Here is an important last word. Every single person in the world is loved by God the same way that you are loved by God. Every person is a one-of-a-kind child (son or daughter) of God. He loves every other person as much as He loves you. God's son, Jesus, died for everyone in the world, not just you.

What difference would it make if you were conscious of this truth next time you are driving in traffic, walking in the mall, or working at the office? What difference would it make to pray, "God, I know that person driving erratically is your son. You created him, know him, and love him. I don't know what is going on in his life today, but I join You in wanting to bless his life. So, Father, would you bless him right now? Would you surround him with Your peace and Your love? If he is under attack of the enemy, I pray against that enemy in Jesus name. I pray for this man's protection from the enemy and that your blessing will surround him. Father, You know and love this man, and because You love him, I choose to love him and bless him in this moment."

Have you ever prayed that way? I am learning to pray for people this way because I am growing in God's love. I am learning to see people differently, more through God's eyes. This is true for my family, friends, church family, people stuck in traffic and store lines, and everyone else. They are all God's beloved children. He is the real creator and true Father of each one of us. If you believe in God's personal love for you, then you need to believe that He has the same love for others. It will change the way you drive. It will change the way you pray for friends and family. It will make you love God even more when you realize how great is His love for all people!

Jesus says that the first and greatest commandment is to love God, and the second is to love people. If you are unclear on who your neighbor might be, Jesus makes this clear in Luke 10:25-37, in the parable about the good Samaritan. We are to love all people, even the different and difficult ones! Go back and read this challenging parable. Jesus wants us to love everyone like that!

When we love God with all our hearts and love people it is because we are growing in the knowledge of His goodness and love. God is good and His love endures forever. God loves you and me more than we can imagine. God has always intended good for your life. Trust Him. Love Him. Walk with Him. Stop hiding and leaving. Stay with Him.

Do you remember the way that I signed the introductory chapter of this book? I called myself "The preacher who Jesus Loves!" I wonder what you thought about my self-proclamation? I preached through John's gospel a few years before I finished writing this book. John called himself "the apostle who Jesus loved" multiple times in the book. Did Jesus actually love John more than He loved Peter, or anybody else, for that matter? I don't believe that Jesus loved John more than anybody else. What was significant was that John knew that Jesus loved him! John's knowledge and trust in Jesus's love for him gave him greater access to Jesus and a deeper level of relationship with Jesus than the other apostles. Peter would try to get John to ask Jesus difficult questions because of John's more intimate relationship. The truth was that the same intimacy that John had with Jesus was available for Peter.

Am I the only preacher who Jesus loves? No. But I am loved by Jesus! I believe it. That belief changes everything. Your knowledge and trust in God's love for you will give you more access to Jesus and will bless you with more relationship with God. You are the _____ (fill in the blank with something unique to you) who He loves! Only you can claim this for your life. When you really believe that it is true, this knowledge and faith will change everything.

The blessings of a healthy Lovelife with God are abundant and eternal. A healthy Lovelife is the most important goal of your life. A healthy Lovelife will bless you in every aspect of your life. Jesus says your Lovelife is most important. Say, "Yes! Jesus." Learn to say, "I trust that you love me Jesus. I love you. You are my life. Without You, I have nothing. With You, I have everything!"

The only thing left is to begin. Reading the book is not enough. Knowing the truths that are in scripture is not enough. It is time for action! Jesus does not tell us to learn about loving God, but He tells us to love God. It is time to begin and then to keep growing in your Lovelife. May God bless you richly as you grow in your love for Him, yourself, and all His children!

LOVELIFE

Chapter 14 - Discussion Questions

1. What are some ways that your Lovelife with God is changing your sense of worth and purpose?

2. What are some ways that your Lovelife is changing the way you love difficult people, the ones that the Bible calls your neighbors?

3. What are some of the times and situations where it is most difficult for you to love people?

4. Can you identify yourself as the _____ who Jesus loves? Talk about your answer.

5. What are some ways that you can begin to love God more today?

Notes

Chapter 6 – The Holy Spirit is More Proof – p59
Tenth Avenue North 2010, "On and On," *The Light Meets the Dark* album, Provident Label Group, Franklin, Tennessee.

Chapter 11 – Learning to Love – p104
Charles Austin Miles, "I Come to the Garden Alone" (No. 595) in *Songs of Faith and Praise* (West Monroe, LA: Howard Publishing Co., INC, 1994)

www.ingramcontent.com/pod-product-compliance
Lightning Source LLC
Chambersburg PA
CBHW032135040426
42449CB00005B/255